Osceola

1804–1838

by *Rachel A. Koestler-Grack*

Content Consultant:
Brent Weisman, author of
Unconquered People: Florida's Seminole
and Miccosukee Indians

Blue Earth Books

an imprint of Capstone Press
Mankato, Minnesota

Blue Earth Books are published by Capstone Press
151 Good Counsel Drive, P.O. Box 669, Mankato, Minnesota 56002
http://www.capstone-press.com

Library of Congress Cataloging-in-Publication Data
Koestler-Grack, Rachel A. 1973–
    Osceola, 1804–1838 / by Rachel A. Koestler-Grack.
        p. cm. — (American Indian biographies)
    Includes bibliographical references and index.
    Summary: Discusses the life of Seminole warrior Osceola, from his childhood in an Upper Creek village
    to his involvement in the Second Seminole War, capture, and death.
    ISBN 0-7368-1211-3 (hardcover)
    1. Osceola, Seminole chief, 1804–1838. 2. Seminole Indians—Biography—Juvenile literature.
3. Seminole Indians—History—Juvenile literature. [1. Osceola, Seminole chief, 1804–1838. 2. Seminole
Indians—Biography. 3. Indians of North America—Florida—Biography. 4. Seminole War, 2nd, 1835–1842.]
    I. Title. II. Series.
    E99.S28 O825 2003
    973'.04973'00—dc21   2001006886

Editorial credits
Editor: Megan Schoeneberger
Cover Designer: Heather Kindseth
Interior Layout Designers: Jennifer Schonborn
    and Heather Kindseth
Interior Illustrator: Jennifer Schonborn
Production Designers: Jennifer Schonborn
    and Gene Bentdahl
Photo Researcher: Mary Englar

Photo credits
Theodore Morris, cover; The Museum of Florida
History, cover (pipe); Art Resource, 5, 8; Library of
Congress, 9; Philbrook Museum, Tulsa, Solomon
McCombs (1957.7), 10, Fred Beaver (1962.7),
12–13, Jerome Tiger (1991.26.2), 14, Fred Beaver
(1957.8), 16; Capstone Press/Gary Sundermeyer, 11,
17; North Wind Picture Archives, 19, 24, 29 (bottom
left, top); Florida State Archives, 21; Hulton/Archive
by Getty Images, 22–23; University of Miami Library
Archives, 25; Courtesy of St. Augustine Historical
Society, 26–27; Capstone Press Archives, 28, 29
(bottom right)

2 3 4 5 6 07 06 05 04 03

Contents

CHAPTER 1
Forced to Leave

Osceola tried to make peace with white people so that the Seminole people could have freedom to live their traditional way of life.

In 1814, the August air was hotter and heavier than Osceola ever remembered. The young American Indian boy had been traveling for weeks with his clan of Upper Creek Indians through the marshy land along the gulf coast of Florida. There was little laughter from the women and children. The men's faces were serious.

Osceola did not know where he was going. All he knew was that his Upper Creek people had lost the war with the white settlers. Now, they must move south. They left their villages, homes, and farmlands in present-day Alabama. The village where he had lived since he was a boy now belonged to the pale-skinned people who called themselves Americans.

On their journey, Osceola and the other Creek walked for many hours each day carrying their belongings. Some people carried bundles of corn and squash. Others toted large baskets filled with clay pots, gardening tools, and beads.

Osceola's Territory in the Early 1800s

SOUTH CAROLINA

Fort Moultrie ▲

ALABAMA

GEORGIA

◇
Osceola's Birthplace

ATLANTIC OCEAN

▲ Fort Scott

Apalachicola River

FLORIDA

▲ Fort King

Withlacoochee River

✕
Osceola's Wartime Village

Legend
▨ Florida Wetlands
▲ Forts
✕ Indian Village

N W E S

Miles
0 25 50 75 100

0 25 50 75 100 125 150
Kilometers

6

Three summers earlier in 1811, a Shawnee Indian named Tecumseh had visited Osceola's Creek people. Tecumseh's mother was a Creek. For this reason, he hoped to gain support from the Upper Creek in creating a united Indian confederacy. As one large nation, the American Indians could fight the whites and keep their land and way of life. Creek warriors from Osceola's village had joined Tecumseh's cause.

Some Creek Indians fought for the British in conflicts against the Americans, including the War of 1812 (1812–1814). The American Indians, led by Tecumseh, believed that the British would help them keep their lands. But the British lost the war, and some Creek lands became the property of the United States.

At age 10, Osceola did not understand how the mighty Creek could be forced off their land. The Creator gave them their land and blessed them with many years of abundant crops. But in the summer of 1814, Osceola's family left their village in Alabama. They moved south and made their homes with the Lower Creek, who lived in northern Florida. The Upper and Lower Creek joined with some people of the native tribes of Florida. Together, they became the Seminole Indians.

In the early 1830s, whites wanted to take Seminole lands in Florida. By this time, Osceola was a grown man and a great war leader among his people. He inspired the Seminole to fight the whites to keep their land and freedom.

Osceola's leadership helped the Seminole preserve their culture. Even though many Seminole people were forced off their lands, not all Seminole surrendered. Today, many Seminole still live in Florida and continue to practice their traditional way of life.

CHAPTER 2

Life in a Creek Village

Around 1804, Osceola was born near the Upper Creek village of Tallassee, near present-day Tuskegee, Alabama. He and his two sisters lived with his mother. Little is known about Osceola's childhood, but he probably was like other Creek boys.

White people later gave Osceola the name Billy Powell, after his father. Some historians believe Osceola's father was a white trader named William Powell. Others do not

American Indian boys learned to hunt at an early age.

Creek Indians in Osceola's village lived in log cabins.

believe this story. Osceola's mother was a Creek Indian. Osceola always considered himself a full-blooded Creek Indian.

Osceola often worked with his mother. He helped her to tend small fields of corn and to plant gardens of beans, squash, pumpkins, and sweet potatoes. Osceola also gathered firewood from nearby forests for the hearth in his family's log home.

In Creek villages, children lived with their mother's families in log cabins. Osceola lived with his uncles and aunts, cousins, and grandparents from his mother's side. Each group of relatives made up a clan. Some clans lived together in villages.

When Osceola was young, he used child-sized weapons to learn how to shoot with a bow and arrows. Osceola quickly became a good marksman. When shooting his arrow, he took careful aim and often hit his target.

Creek boys played sports and games in their free time. Many of these games improved their strength and endurance. Osceola wrestled with other Creek boys and competed in foot races. At special celebrations, Osceola and other boys played ball game. During this game, players threw a deerskin ball at a target that had been secured to the top of a tall pole.

When Osceola was 9 years old, warriors in his Upper Creek village prepared to battle the Americans. But the U.S. Army quickly defeated the Upper Creek warriors. If Osceola's family wanted to keep their freedom, they needed to journey south to find a new home.

A ball game target sometimes was the skull of a bull cow. Other times, the Seminole used a carved fish shape as the target.

Play Ball Game

What You Need

newspapers

piece of wood, cut about 10 inches by 10 inches
  (25 centimeters by 25 centimeters), could be
  cut in the shape of a cow's head or a fish

acrylic paints

paintbrushes

tree

nails

hammer

ladder

paper

pencil or pen

brick, piece of wood, or some other marker
  to use as a throw line

small wooden ball

What You Do

1. Spread the newspapers on a table. Use the paints to decorate the wooden target.

2. Ask an adult to nail the wooden target into a tree about 20 feet (6 meters) from the ground.

3. Decide which player will keep track of points. This player should write each player's name on a sheet of paper.

4. Place the throw line marker 5 feet (1.5 meters) from the base of the tree.

5. Each player takes three turns throwing the wooden ball at the target. When throwing the ball, each player should stand at the throw line. Players who are not throwing should stand at least 10 feet (3 meters) behind the thrower. This action will protect other players from accidentally being hit by the ball.

6. A player receives four points for hitting the target. If the ball hits the tree within about 3 feet (1 meter) of the target, the player receives two points.

7. At the end of three rounds, the player with the most points wins the game.

CHAPTER 3
Growing Up Seminole

When Osceola's people reached northern Florida, they lived near another group of native people called the Lower Creek. The Lower Creek welcomed Osceola's Upper Creek people. White people called this group of American Indians "Seminoles." This name was taken from the Spanish word cimmarrones, meaning "wild ones."

Osceola helped his family build a new house. The land in Florida was swampy in some areas. Streams often flooded from frequent rains. As they moved farther south, the Seminole began to build huts on stiltlike legs to keep their homes dry

Chickees were practical in the swampy lands of Florida. Though their clothing changed, many Seminole continued to live in chickees well into the 1900s.

during times of flooding. They called these houses "chickees," the Seminole word for house. Each chickee had a thatched roof made of palmetto leaves. The thick roof kept the chickee dry during heavy rainstorms.

Seminole men often fished from dugout canoes.

Osceola helped his mother plant fields of corn, squash, and beans on hammocks. These small patches of fertile land were ideal for farming. The men in his village fished in nearby streams. In surrounding forests, Seminole men hunted deer, rabbits, and bears. Before long, Osceola's family learned to survive in their new lands.

At night, Osceola and other children gathered around the fire to listen to the elders tell stories. Seminole people believed that the Creator made animals with supernatural powers. Many stories were about animals and taught lessons about respecting nature.

When Osceola was 15 years old, he began preparing for an important event. During the Green Corn Dance celebration, Osceola would join other Seminole men in the sacred cleansing ceremony. He would be accepted as an adult member of the village.

Osceola helped his village get ready for the Green Corn Dance celebration. He gathered firewood for the dance fires with his mother and aunts. He went hunting with other men in his tribe. Clans gathered at sacred ceremonial grounds.

On the first day of the Green Corn Dance, the men built a large fire in the center of the camp. Throughout the celebration, they would keep this fire burning. Many smaller cook fires also were lit around the camps. Smoke hung above the camp in the thick, humid air.

During the first two days of the Green Corn Dance, Osceola fasted.

By not eating any food, Osceola purified his body for his sacred passage into adulthood. Seminole warriors also fasted. Osceola probably felt honored to be participating in this ceremony with other adult members of his tribe.

Osceola still fasted the third day of the celebration. He danced around the fires, keeping his mind focused on the sacred celebration. He closed his eyes and let the jumping flames of the dance fire warm his skin.

The men took turns scooping ladles of a bitter black drink called asi. After swallowing the sacred drink, they found a private place to vomit. The Seminole performed this ritual to purify themselves.

At midnight, Osceola stood with the other young men in his tribe. The dance leader picked up his rattle, signaling the beginning of the Green Corn Dance. They sang songs to the

Creator. Some boys drank the asi drink. Others rubbed the liquid over their bodies. Osceola and the other boys then danced around the fire.

On the fourth day of the Green Corn Dance, the villagers prepared to feast. Women boiled sofki. Osceola often ate this cornmeal soup with his family. Clans gathered around a large sofki bowl. Each clan member ate several spoonfuls of the soup and passed the sofki spoon to the next person. After the feast, Seminole clans returned to their villages.

The Green Corn Dance celebration is an ancient tradition for American Indians of the Southeast.

16

Pumpkin Bread Cakes

Osceola's mother and aunts may have made pumpkin bread cakes for the Green Corn Dance. The Seminole often served this traditional food at celebrations.

What You Need

Ingredients

4 cups (1,000 mL) self-rising flour

1 cup (250 mL) sugar

1 15-ounce (450-gram) can of plain pumpkin

1 cup (250 mL) all-purpose flour for kneading

1 cup (250 mL) canola oil

¼ cup (50 mL) sugar, for topping

Equipment

measuring cups	large frying pan
large bowl	spatula
wooden spoon	paper towels
liquid measuring cup	

What You Do

1. Mix together flour and sugar in a large bowl.
2. Add pumpkin. Stir until all of the flour is mixed into the pumpkin and forms a soft dough ball.
3. Sprinkle a small amount of flour on top of the dough ball. Over the bowl, rub a small amount of flour between your hands.
4. Gently knead the dough, pushing it with the heels of your hands.
5. Fold the dough in half.
6. Sprinkle more flour on top of the dough to keep it from sticking to your hands. Knead and fold several times, adding more flour each time you knead.
7. Take a piece of dough about the size of your palm and shape it into a patty. Keep making patties until all dough has been used.
8. Heat oil in frying pan on medium heat.
9. When oil is hot, gently fill frying pan with patties.
10. Cook patties several minutes and turn each with a spatula.
11. Cook about four minutes longer.
12. Remove the patties from pan. Place them on several layers of paper towels to drain and cool. Cook the remaining patties.
13. Sprinkle remaining sugar over the top of each cake.

Makes about 20 cakes

CHAPTER 4
Finding Peace

Seminole warriors hid and then attacked a U.S. supply boat in an ambush on the Apalachicola River.

As an adult member of his village, Osceola began accompanying other men on hunting parties and war parties. In the First Seminole War (1817–1818), the Seminole fought against the U.S. government. In November 1817, Osceola and other Seminole warriors attacked a U.S. Army boat while it was traveling up the Apalachicola River in northern Florida. The boat was carrying supplies to Fort Scott near present-day Reynoldsville, Georgia. The Seminole warriors took a white woman captive during this attack.

In the spring of 1818, U.S. soldiers went in search of the group of Seminole who had taken the white woman prisoner. The soldiers found the warriors and rescued the white woman, taking some of the warriors as prisoners. Among the prisoners taken was 14-year-old Osceola. He was later released.

As Osceola grew older, he became a strong warrior and capable leader. In Seminole culture, most chiefs inherited the position of chief from relatives on

their mother's side. Osceola's ancestors were not chiefs. So Osceola never became a Seminole chief. But he had incredible war and leadership skills. Many Seminole people followed Osceola because they trusted his abilities as a warrior.

In the late 1820s or early 1830s, Osceola married Chechoter, a Creek woman whose name meant "the morning dew." Historians believe Chechoter also had African ancestors. Little is known about their marriage. But they had a daughter and perhaps another child.

In the spring of 1835, government officials visited the Seminole villages. They wanted to control Seminole lands. If the Seminole agreed to leave their land, the Americans promised them a piece of land in Indian Territory, in present-day Oklahoma. Osceola feared that if the Seminole left their land, they would lose their freedom and be unable to practice their traditional way of life.

Osceola convinced the Seminole Chief Micanopy to refuse to leave Seminole land. "The white man wants to stomp out the Seminole like a pile of burning leaves," Osceola told his friend.

A government official named Wiley Thompson asked Seminole leaders to come to nearby Fort King. He wanted the chiefs to sign a treaty, or agreement, promising to leave the land.

Some Seminole leaders made their signature mark on the treaty. Most Seminole did not speak English or spell their names. They drew a simple *X* as their signature. Chief Micanopy did not sign the treaty.

Osceola was present at the treaty talk. According to one story, Osceola walked through the crowd of Seminole to the table where the treaty lay. He pulled his knife from its sheath and stabbed it through the treaty papers.

"This is my mark," Osceola told the white soldiers. "I will make no other."

About a week later in early June, white soldiers captured Osceola and took him to Fort King. Thompson held Osceola as a prisoner until he signed the treaty. After two days, Osceola agreed to sign the treaty and help Thompson move the Seminole to Indian Territory.

Osceola began visiting Fort King frequently. Osceola became well liked and trusted by the whites at Fort King. For the next several months, Osceola helped Thompson keep peace between the white settlers and the Seminole.

According to legend, Osceola stuck his knife through treaty papers. He refused to sign the agreement to give up claims to Seminole lands.

During his visits to Fort King, Osceola became friends with a white officer named John Graham. The two men were often seen together. Osceola sometimes brought his daughter to Fort King. Graham was kind to the girl and sometimes gave her gifts. In return, Osceola presented Graham with a plume of white crane feathers to wear if the whites should ever battle the Seminole. The feathers were a signal to Seminole warriors that this man was a friend.

CHAPTER 5
A War Leader

Osceola quickly became a respected member of the Seminole people. Many Seminole told Osceola about problems with white settlers. Osceola then spoke to Wiley Thompson, who tried to solve the problems. The Seminole trusted Osceola, who was always bold and firm in his requests. Thompson also trusted Osceola. As a token of friendship, Thompson gave Osceola a silver-plated rifle.

During the fall of 1835, relations between white settlers and Seminole villagers became strained. A group of white settlers attacked a Seminole hunting party for traveling outside territory boundaries that had been set by the U.S. Army. A Seminole hunter was killed during the fight. This event angered Osceola, who blamed Thompson for the Seminole hunter's death.

On the afternoon of December 28, 1835, Osceola took about 60 warriors to Fort King. The warriors hid behind trees in the nearby forest. Thompson and a

The Seminole often surrounded and attacked U.S. forts in battles to keep the government from taking their land.

guest were enjoying an after-dinner walk around the fort walls. Osceola took careful aim at Thompson and shot. Thompson fell to the ground, killed by the very gun he had given to Osceola as a gift.

Osceola then gave a shrill war whoop. At this signal, the warriors ran out from their hiding spots and charged the fort. The warriors killed Thompson's companion and several other people at Fort King before they slipped back into the woods. Meanwhile, another group of warriors led by Chief Micanopy attacked a party of soldiers on the Fort King Road south of the fort.

These events triggered the start of the Second Seminole War (1835–1842). A month after his attack on Fort King, Osceola led a group of warriors in battle against U.S. soldiers who were searching for Seminole Indians. The battle took place near the

Withlacoochee River. Osceola's warriors defeated the soldiers. After this battle, Osceola promised, "I will fight until the last drop of Seminole blood has moistened the dust of my hunting ground."

Seminole warriors sometimes used fire as a weapon to attack and destroy U.S. forts during the Second Seminole War.

Osceola led several battles against the American soldiers during the Second Seminole War. He proved to be a wise war leader. He helped plot successful ambushes of white soldiers.

The war made life difficult for Seminole villagers. They often had to move their villages to keep hidden from American soldiers. Oftentimes, they did not stay in one place long enough to plant and harvest crops. Their food supply became scarce. The Seminole people wanted to live in peace.

Osceola became a great war leader for the Seminole people.

CHAPTER 6

Under a Flag of Truce

♦ ♦ ♦ ————————

"My head is just like before. You haven't won."
—Osceola at his capture in 1837

Osceola's warriors were becoming tired of fighting. Osceola had become sick with malaria and was weak. The Seminole people wanted to keep their villages in peace, planting crops and living in the ways of their ancestors. Osceola decided to talk about making peace with the whites.

In October 1837, a general named Thomas Jesup sent other officers to talk to Osceola and the Seminole chiefs. The Seminole agreed to meet with the officers under a white flag of truce. The flag meant that the leaders of both sides could talk about peace without fighting.

Osceola (center holding flag) was captured under a flag of truce and taken prisoner.

As the officers neared Osceola, he noticed them raise their guns. Some soldiers grabbed Osceola and took him prisoner. Osceola must have been angry at himself for trusting these men. They betrayed him.

One of the soldiers who grabbed Osceola shouted, "You thought I wouldn't win, but this time I win. I've captured you."

"No," Osceola said. "My head is just like before. You haven't won."

Jesup sent Osceola as a prisoner to Fort Moultrie in South Carolina. At the fort, Osceola could not practice his traditional way of life. While he was prisoner, Osceola's malaria worsened.

White doctors wanted to treat Osceola's disease. But Osceola would not let them. Instead, he used Seminole medicines to treat his illness.

Osceola became much weaker within a few months. He felt as though his life was near its end. Osceola painted half of his face red to show the Creator he was ready to die.

On January 30, 1838, Osceola dressed in brightly colored clothing and draped jewelry around his neck. He lay down on his bed. Osceola clutched his knife across his chest and took his final breath.

Osceola was buried at Fort Moultrie in South Carolina.

Chronology

1814

Osceola's Upper Creek village is forced out of Alabama. They move to northern Florida.

December 1835

Osceola leads a group of Seminole warriors during an attack on Wiley Thompson at Fort King.

June 1835

Osceola is taken prisoner at Fort King. He is released after two days.

October 1837

Osceola is taken prisoner under a flag of truce, while discussing peace with the whites.

About 1804

Osceola is born.

1817

Osceola participates in an ambush of a U.S. supply ship on its way to Fort Scott.

January 30, 1838

Osceola dies of malaria while he is a prisoner at Fort Moultrie in South Carolina.

Words to Know

abundant (uh-BUN-duhnt)—plenty or a great amount of something

ambush (AM-bush)—a sudden, surprise attack

ancestor (AN-sess-tur)—a member of a family or a relation who lived long ago

betray (bi-TRAY)—to be disloyal to someone by a deed that hurts that person

elder (EL-dur)—an older person; in American Indian tribes, an elder was an older, respected, and knowledgeable member of the village.

fertile (FUR-tuhl)—rich or productive; soil that is fertile is good for growing crops.

hearth (HARTH)—the area in front of a fireplace

malaria (muh-LAIR-ee-ah)—a serious disease that people get from mosquito bites; malaria causes high fever, chills, and sometimes death.

palmetto (pal-MET-oh)—a type of palm tree with leaves shaped like fans

purify (PYOOR-uh-fye)—to make something pure or clean

sheath (SHEETH)—a cover or holder for a knife

surrender (suh-REN-dur)—to give up, or to admit that you are beaten in a battle

tote (TOHT)—to carry or haul something

treaty (TREE-tee)—a formal agreement between two or more governing groups

trigger (TRIG-ur)—to cause something to happen as a reaction

truce (TROOSS)—an agreement to stop fighting while peace is discussed

To Learn More

Bial, Raymond. *The Seminole.* Lifeways. New York: Benchmark Books, 2000.

Englar, Mary. *The Seminole: The First People of Florida.* American Indian Nations. Mankato, Minn.: Bridgestone Books, 2003.

Sonneborn, Liz. *The Seminole.* Watts Library. New York: Franklin Watts, 2002.

Yacowitz, Caryn. *The Seminole.* Native Americans. Chicago: Heinemann Library, 2002.

Internet Sites

Fort Moultrie: Osceola
http://www.nps.gov/fosu/sb/osceola

Seminoles of Florida History
http://dhr.dos.state.fl.us/flafacts/seminole.html

The Seminole Tribe of Florida
http://www.seminoletribe.com

The Seminole Wars
http://dhr.dos.state.fl.us/flafacts/semwar.html

Places to Visit

Ah-Tah-Thi-Ki Museum
Big Cypress Reservation
HC-61
P.O. Box 21-A
Clewiston, FL 33440

Dade Battlefield Historic State Park
7200 CR 603
Bushnell, FL 33513

Fort Moultrie
1214 Middle Street
Sullivan's Island, SC 29482

Seminole Nation Museum
524 South Wewoka Avenue
P.O. Box 532
Wewoka, OK 74884

Index